My Life in an
ALGONQUIAN VILLAGE

By Lynda Arnéz

Please visit our website, www.garethstevens.com. For a free color catalog of all our high-quality books, call toll free 1-800-542-2595 or fax 1-877-542-2596.

Library of Congress Cataloging-in-Publication Data

Arnéz, Lynda.
  My life in an Algonquian village / Lynda Arnéz.
      pages cm — (My place in history)
  Includes index.
  ISBN 978-1-4824-3984-7 (pbk.)
  ISBN 978-1-4824-3985-4 (6 pack)
  ISBN 978-1-4824-3986-1 (library binding)
  1. Algonquian Indians—Social life and customs. I. Title.
  E99.A35A76 2016
  973.04'973—dc23

                              2015021464

First Edition

Published in 2016 by
Gareth Stevens Publishing
111 East 14th Street, Suite 349
New York, NY 10003

Copyright © 2016 Gareth Stevens Publishing

Designer: Laura Bowen
Editor: Kristen Nelson

Photo credits: Cover, p. 1 (village) Tungsten/Wikimedia Commons; cover, pp. 1-24 (torn strip) barbaliss/Shutterstock.com; cover, pp. 1-24 (photo frame) Davor Ratkovic/Shutterstock.com; cover, pp. 1-24 (white paper) HABRDA/Shutterstock.com; cover, pp. 1-24 (parchment) M. Unal Ozmen/Shutterstock.com; cover, pp. 1-24 (textured edge) saki80/Shutterstock.com; cover (background) Natalia Sheinkin/Shutterstock.com; pp. 1-24 (paper background) Kostenko Maxim/Shutterstock.com; p. 5 (map) ish ishwar/Wikimedia Commons; p. 5 (chief) Bkwillwm/Wikimedia Commons; p. 7 (main) Kordas/ Wikimedia Commons; p. 9 (main) Three Lions/Hulton Archive/Getty Images; p. 9 (inset) MPI/Archive Photos/Getty Images; p. 11 (main) DEA Picture Library/De Agostini/Getty Images; p. 11 (inset) Fourinthemorning/Wikimedia Commons; p. 13 (Algonquian couple) Poisend Ivy/Wikimedia Commons; p. 13 (fish) Marilyn Angel Wynn/Nativestock/Getty Images; p. 13 (hide) Stacey Newman/Shutterstock.com; p. 14 (inset) Rob at Houghton/Wikimedia Commons; p. 15 (main) Perry Thorsvik/ America 24-7/Getty Images; p. 17 (main) Theodore de Bry/Getty Images; p. 17 (inset) Stock Montage/Archive Photos/ Getty Images; p. 19 (main) General Photographic Agency/Hulton Archive/Getty Images; p. 19 (inset) Hulton Archive/ Getty Images; p. 21 Kean Collection/Archive Photos/Getty Images.

Printed in the United States of America

CPSIA compliance information: Batch #CW16GS: For further information contact Gareth Stevens, New York, New York at 1-800-542-2595.

CONTENTS

Words in the glossary appear in **bold** type the first time they are used in the text.

A new LANGUAGE

May 1, 1609

   This is my first time writing in English on my own! My cousin Namontack went to live with the English last year to learn more about them. He's been teaching me how to speak and write like the people in Jamestown since he got back. I wish I could go see the fort like some of the **warriors** have.

   My mother says Chief Wahunsonacock (wah-huhn-SEHN-uh-kawh) shouldn't trust the English. I'm not worried. He brought more than 30 tribes together to make our strong **confederacy**!

Notes from History

The confederacy created by Chief Wahunsonacock was in present-day Virginia. The English called Wahunsonacock by the name Powhatan and his people the Powhatans.

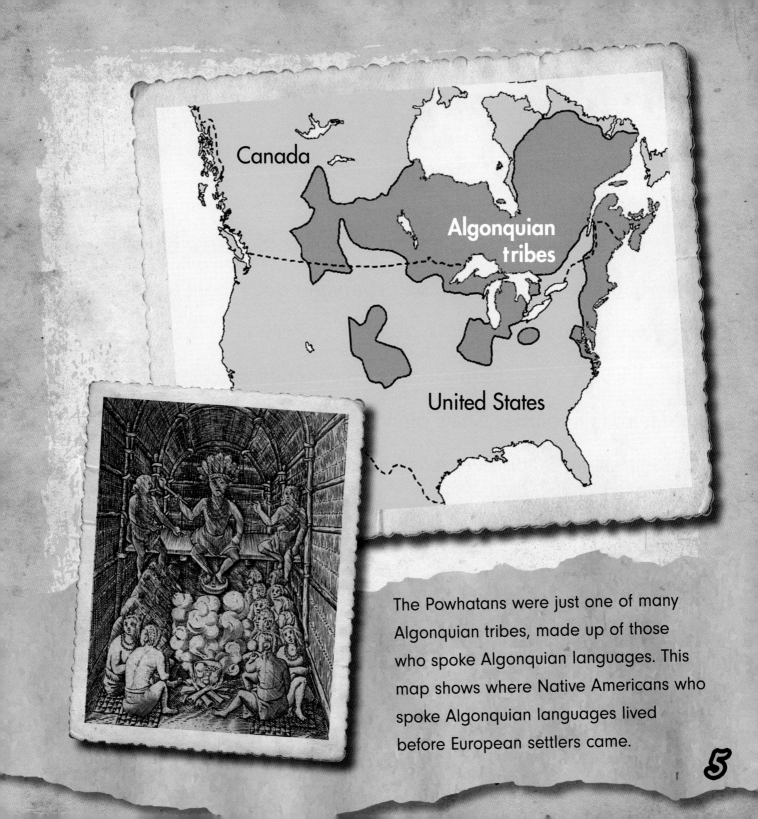

Canada

Algonquian
tribes

United States

The Powhatans were just one of many Algonquian tribes, made up of those who spoke Algonquian languages. This map shows where Native Americans who spoke Algonquian languages lived before European settlers came.

Women's WORK

June 4, 1609

My sisters and I just got back from bathing in the river. Our home is so close to it, and everyone goes there to wash in the morning.

It's very warm here today, so my mother is rolling up the sides of our *yehakin*. She's planning on gathering more bark and small trees today to fix some **damage** that happened during last week's rainstorm. My sisters are heading to the fields with some of the other women. What will I do?

Notes from History

Groups of Powhatans lived together on waterways in Virginia, including the York River, James River, and Potomac River.

Powhatan women built and took care of the *yehakins*, the small homes made of young trees and bark the tribe lived in.

Washington, DC

Maryland

Chesapeake Bay

Powhatan territory, 1607

Virginia

North Carolina

Growing Up POWHATAN

When my father is home, I go with him and the other boys to fish or hunt nearby. I'm getting better with my bow and arrow! But some of the men, including my father, are away watching the Englishmen at Jamestown. They're ready to attack if they need to.

My mother says I'll be with her today! While she gathers bark for the *yehakin*, I'm going to look for fruit and nuts for us to eat. I might go out to help in the fields, too.

Notes from History

Around age 15, boys were considered men in Powhatan society. Then, they would hunt and go to war more often than help at home.

In 1609, the Powhatans and English were still often friendly. However, as Jamestown grew, the two groups fought more.

What's for DINNER?

August 10, 1609

I spent a long time in the fields today! The corn has already grown so tall. I ate a few late beans right from the plant, and they were so sweet! They'll taste good with the fish my father brought back with him this morning.

After dinner, I have to help my mother **tan** some animal **hides** to make new clothes. In the summer, I don't wear much of anything! But once winter comes, we all need to wear the deerskin clothes my mother makes.

Notes from History

It's likely that the Powhatans hunted more in the fall and winter. Powhatan men used bows and arrows to hunt deer and traps to catch smaller animals like beavers.

Algonquians living on waterways traveled in canoes somewhat like this one.

Fun and CELEBRATION

I have a little time to play with my friends today. We're going to race! I'm one of the fastest runners of all the boys. My father says this will make me a good hunter someday—and being a good hunter means being a good warrior!

One of the oldest warriors in our village died this week. We're going to celebrate his life tonight! There's going to be a feast, dancing, and music. We have songs and dances for just about every occasion.

Notes from History

Powhatans made **instruments** from turtle shells and animal skins stretched to make drums.

Like today, Powhatans celebrated marriages. Before marrying a woman, a man might bring her family fish he caught or the hide of an animal he killed to prove he could provide for her.

September 30, 1609

A big group of visitors came to our village today! They're part of the Kuskarawaok people. They live on a river, too, and have canoes to travel on the water, like we do. They brought nets and spears for fishing along the way.

The Kuskarawaok speak the same language we do. I talked to a young Kuskarawaok warrior. He said his people have met the English, too! A man named Captain John Smith was exploring near their village, and they traded with him.

CAPTAIN JOHN SMITH

14

The Kuskarawaoks, or Nanticokes, were an Algonquian tribe that lived on the Nanticoke River in the early 1600s. They were **allies** of the Powhatans.

The Nanticokes lived in present-day Maryland and Delaware. They lived in wigwams, which were built of branches, vines, and hide, and were somewhat similar to *yehakins*.

Algonquians TO THE NORTH

October 15, 1609

I've been thinking about what the Kuskarawaok warrior told me. He said there are even more tribes north of us that speak the same kind of language we do! He's visited the Wabanaki, the Wampanoag, the Lenni Lenape, and many more.

Some of these tribes live in longhouses that as many as 60 people can live in! It snows a lot in some of those places, so they wear furs to stay warm. I'd like to visit other tribes and learn about them someday!

Notes from History

The Wampanoag are the Algonquian tribe who met the Pilgrims at Plymouth in Massachusetts in 1620.

LONGHOUSE

Algonquian tribes also lived south of the Powhatans. These images show what other Native American villages of the time might have looked like.

17

Wish to See THE WORLD

November 1, 1609

Some of my father's family lives in the Kuskarawaok village our visitors are from! Once he and my mother got married, he moved to her village.

I told my father I want to meet people from different tribes like ours. He's been talking to the Kuskarawaok leaders about me! He said I might be able to go back to their village when they leave. He can't come with me because our chief needs all the men in his **siege** of Jamestown.

Notes from History

The winter of 1609 and 1610 is called the Starving Time in the history of Jamestown. The Powhatans surrounded the settlement and wouldn't let food or supplies in!

JAMESTOWN, 1610

Many Native American tribes, including the Powhatans, are matrilineal. This means family is traced through a person's mother.

November 10, 1609

Dear Mother and Father,

    I have just arrived at the Kuskarawaok village. After leaving home with the group of warriors, we paddled a long way in their canoes. I met Father's family right away! Did you know he's **related** to the chief here?

    I'm already learning a lot. The chief said I can go with him when he visits their close neighbors, the Lenape and Munsee tribes. When I come back to our village next year, I will have met so many people from different tribes!

Notes from History

Most Algonquian tribes didn't have any form of writing.

Lenni Lenape

New Jersey and Pennsylvania

Powhatans

Virginia

Mahicans

New York

Lumbee

North Carolina

Who are Algonquian tribes?

any Native American group that speaks an Algonquian language

Shawnee

Ohio

Wampanoag

Massachusetts and Rhode Island

Nanticoke

Maryland and Delaware

GLOSSARY

ally: one of two or more groups that help each other

confederacy: a league of groups joined together for a purpose, such as protection

damage: harm

hide: the skin of an animal

instrument: an object used to make music

related: connected by family

siege: the use of military to surround an area or building in order to capture it

tan: to change an animal skin into leather

warrior: one who fights

For more INFORMATION

Books

Collinson, Clare, ed. *Peoples of the East, Southeast, and Plains*. Redding, CT: Brown Bear Books, 2009.

Cunningham, Kevin, and Peter Benoit. *The Wampanoag*. New York, NY: Children's Press, 2011.

Yasuda, Anita. *Explore Native American Cultures*. White River Junction, VT: Nomad Press, 2013.

Websites

Facts for Kids: Algonquian Indian Tribes
www.bigorrin.org/algonquian_kids.htm
There's a lot to learn about the Algonquian group! Find out more here.

Native Americans: Tribes and Regions
www.ducksters.com/history/native_american_tribes_regions.php
Find out much more about the Native Americans of North America.

INDEX